INSTRUCTIONAL UNIT PLAN

DANA GIOIA

Wiseblood Books
P.O. Box 870
Menomonee Falls, WI 53052

Printed in the United States of America

Set in Calluna Typesetting
Cover Design: Louis Maltese

ISBN 13: Paperback: 978-1-963319-97-2

Wiseblood Books

THE LIVING FIRE

Contemporary Catholic Writers
for the Classroom

Instructional Unit Plan: Dana Gioia

Edited by Sarah Cortez & Lesley Clinton

WISEBLOOD BOOKS

CONTENTS

PREFACE

We are delighted that you have chosen to enhance your educational toolkit with this unit plan from *The Living Fire: Contemporary Catholic Writers in the Classroom* series. The poets featured in this curriculum write with a sacramental view of our world, and their works offer us a chance to discover—or rediscover—the enchanting, incarnational joy of poetry. Thank you for nourishing your students' intellectual and spiritual growth by introducing them to these vibrant works by Catholic poets of our time.

In each lesson plan, we have sought to provide you with options. You will most likely find more material than you can cover in a single class session. Use whichever of the resources and activities you feel will best meet your course's learning objectives. You'll find vocabulary to scaffold reading comprehension, as well as challenges for advanced students and activities that appeal to different learning styles. You'll also find critical thinking discussion questions with suggested responses or considerations. Students can explore these questions in many ways, including through teacher-led discussion, think-pair-share, small group work, individual written response, or student-led seminars.

Although analysis can enrich our experience of a poem, we urge you to prioritize enjoyment when encountering any poem with your students. To this end we have included, along with resources for literary analysis, suggestions for more experiential activities such as memorization and performance. We hope these embodied poetic experiences will benefit your classroom and open your students' hearts to the great joy of poetry.

Lesley Clinton and Sarah Cortez

The Series Editors

LESSON ONE

ANSWERING GOD'S INVITATION

"Finding a Box of Family Letters"
&
"The Burning Ladder"

Objectives

1. Evaluate details in a poem to analyze key ideas.

2. Analyze characterization, point of view, and plot in a poem.

3. Compose a poem using indirect characterization, alliteration, and sensory details.

4. Apply narrative elements and plot details from a scripture passage to an original poem.

5. Use dialogue to contribute to characterization.

Overview

This lesson encourages students to participate in the delight of storytelling, the use of multi-generational wisdom-sharing, and the choice of vivid details for characterization.

Memorization and Recitation

Dana Gioia has called for a return to the sensory pleasure of reciting memorized poetry. "The power of poetry," he says, "is to affect the emotions, touch the memory, and incite the imagination with unusual force."[1] Gioia's innovative program Poetry Out Loud, sponsored by the National Endowment for the Arts during his tenure as director, has engaged millions of high school students across America in the rewarding experience of memorizing and reciting poetry. Gioia says:

> The best way to engage the imagination of students is to augment critical analysis with experiential, performative, and creative forms of knowledge. Memorization and recitation should be restored as foundational techniques.[2]

Prepare students for the culminating activity of this unit: a recitation of one Dana Gioia poem. On the last day of the unit, each student will present the chosen poem for the class. Have each student pick one poem from the unit. The students' homework will be to memorize a fourth of the poem each night. Counsel those who are anxious about memorization to select a shorter poem and encourage them with positive thinking! For now, have students read their poems aloud to a partner. Clarify that the goal of this first reading aloud is simply to enjoy the sounds of the poem.

Essential Questions

"Finding a Box of Family Letters"

☐ *Who is the speaker in this poem? Why does the speaker describe the father as "so young and handsome"? Why is the speaker heartbroken to see his father this way?*

☐ *What advice do you think someone from the past might give you today?*

☐ *How can gratitude help us make the most of each day we have been given?*

☐ *How might a poet use a physical object to anchor abstract reflection in the real world?*

☐ *How can a poet depict the past, present, and future in the space of a single poem?*

"The Burning Ladder"

- *Why did the poet choose Jacob's story to write about?*

- *If God were calling you to a great mission today, what might it be?*

- *When God invites us to wonder, adventure, and mystery, why do we often hesitate to respond?*

- *How can line length contribute to meaning in a poem?*

- *How might a poet use sensory details to convey internal conflict?*

Literary Devices Introduced in This Lesson

ALLITERATION—repeated initial sound

DIALOGUE—a conversation between two people in a book, poem, or play

DICTION—the author's word choice in a piece of writing

FIGURATIVE LANGUAGE—language that is not meant to be taken literally

SENSORY DETAIL—language that appeals to the five senses

SIMILE—the comparison of two things using "like" or "as"

SPEAKER—the imaginary voice speaking the words of a poem

"Finding a Box of Family Letters"

Do you know the meaning of the phrase *carpe diem* from Horace's *Odes*? We normally hear this phrase translated as "seize the day," implying boldly taking advantage of opportunities and making the most of our time. But as Latin scholar Maria S. Marsilio points out, "'carpe diem' is . . . more accurately translated as 'plucking the day,' evoking the gathering of ripening fruits or flowers, enjoying a moment that is rooted in the sensory experience of nature."[3]

Vocabulary

Sentimental—emotional, sappy

Tedious—dull or monotonous

Body of the Lesson

Read aloud "Finding a Box of Family Letters," then give students a few minutes to circle words or phrases that they find striking. Invite a few students to share their words and phrases. Ask them to explain what they find interesting about their selections. Next, have students identify sound devices and literary devices in the poem. Discuss the effects of these devices, with an emphasis on how they contribute to mood, tone, and characterization.

Can you find any alliteration in this poem? Examples of alliteration include: "sentence sounds"; "large, long"; "reeks of regret"; "courthouse clock"; "rounds, routine"; "too tedious"; "silly, sentimental"; "simple-minded to miss"; and "we will be."

Where does Gioia use assonance in this poem? Examples of assonance include: "old post"; "when ended"; and "never let us forget."

What is the effect of alliteration and assonance in the poem? The *s*, *m*, and *r* alliterative sounds and the assonance of the short *e* and long *o* create a contemplative mood. In contrast, the *c* sound works to convey time's mechanical march.

FIGURATIVE LANGUAGE

What is the effect of the simile in the poem? The simile "There is a large, long photograph / curled like a diploma" suggests both a historic accomplishment viewed with pride and expectations for the future.

How do the positive connotations of "diploma" contrast the "regret" mentioned at the end of the stanza? What might be the effect of this ironic contrast in tone? This shift in tone from accomplished to regretful reminds us that sometimes life doesn't meet our expectations.

The first character introduced in this poem is the speaker's father. Which details build a picture of this man? Do you know what he looked like and accomplished? The speaker describes his father in the photo as "young and handsome," with "jet-black hair," standing in "his navy uniform / grinning beside his dive bomber." He was also well-travelled. In his letters he writes from places the speaker "never knew he saw."

How does the speaker show the parents' era through details? We envision the parents' era through the banquet hall, references to waltz and foxtrot, penny stamps, and the old courthouse clock.

How might "A penny stamp" mean more than its primary meaning? What other figurative images are employed? The penny stamp reflects an era in America when many items were less expensive to purchase and many citizens held homespun values such as thriftiness, patriotism, and faith in God.

DIALOGUE

Whose voices do we hear in this poem? The speaker seems to be a son or daughter who might be characterized as reminiscent and pensive, missing the father. The parents urge the speaker (and us), "Get out there on the floor and dance! / You don't have forever."

Notice that this encouragement to dance is repeated at the end of the poem. Why is this urgent message emphasized by repetition? We can read this imperative literally, referring to "getting out there on the dance floor," or figuratively, meaning that we should live life with gratitude for each moment and with appreciation for our loved ones.

"Love always. Can't wait to get home." And *"See you there." Who says these lines?* The speaker's deceased loved ones in letters from the past speak these words.

NARRATIVE

Why did the poet primarily use present tense verbs to tell this story? As the speaker looks through old pictures and reads letters, the past comes alive, and the voices of the deceased seem immediate and present. Their messages feel urgent and significant.

METAPHOR

Where is home? Home can serve as a metaphor for heaven, where we will live in the joy of God's kingdom. We are urged not to regret but to *"carpe diem"* in the real sense, to pluck the bountiful harvest of this mortal life, including our joyful moments with loved ones, by facing them with gratitude and wonder. The habits of gratitude and wonder draw us closer to God and to a joyful eternity with our loved ones.

"The Burning Ladder"

Context Setting

Now we'll look at a poem that examines the challenge of following God's call, of getting out on the floor and dancing.

A pilgrim is someone who makes a journey for a religious purpose, typically to a holy place. Joshua Hren says, "As St. Augustine writes in *The City of God*, the Christian, as a citizen of heaven, is ever-cognizant of his status as *civitas peregrine* (XVIII, 1, 3). In other words, in this world subjects of God are 'resident strangers'... almost a passing stranger in the comfortable, settled life around him."[4] In what ways might you call yourself a pilgrim?

Vocabulary

Seraphim—angels of the highest order

Body of the Lesson

Read aloud "The Burning Ladder" and, if time permits, Genesis 28: 10-22, the scripture passage to which this poem alludes. Have students identify and discuss figurative language, sound devices, imagery, and narrative features of the poem.

FIGURATIVE LANGUAGE

Consider the simile in the line "Sleep / pressed him like a stone." What does this simile suggest? The comparison to sleep and the weight of a stone suggests exhaustion and a heavy burden.

How do the similes in this poem use contrasts to create meaning? The contrast between being pressed "like a stone / in the dust" and rising "like a flame to join / that choir" emphasizes the freedom, adventure, and excitement of a life aligned with God's will.

SOUND DEVICES

Can you find a thematic connection among words in the poem that contribute to alliteration and assonance? The poet uses alliteration of *s* sounds in many of the poem's most important words to convey Jacob's spiritual pilgrimage: *sleep, stone, sick, Seraphim, steps, stars, slept, shivering.* Assonance connects physical realities with emotional realities in word pairings such as *distances / missed* and *ladder / scattered.*

IMAGERY

Why does the speaker characterize the ladder as "burning" in line 3? How does "burning" continue in the reader's imagination through the words and images of the poem? The ladder burns like desire, or passion, or a burning building, or perhaps like the bush that Moses saw burning unconsumed with sacred fire. The simile "risen / like a flame" carries the image, as does the "scattered light."

NARRATIVE

Why doesn't Jacob climb the ladder? He's tired and "sick of travelling," "gravity / always greater than desire."

Does the poem give any hints about how the speaker views Jacob's decision not to climb the ladder? The speaker emphasizes all that Jacob misses and seems to portray the decision as a failure to live fully. For example, while he sleeps, Jacob closes his eyes to glories such as the "Seraphim / ascending . . ."

How does Jacob's sleep represent our failure to respond to God's callings? Does Jacob fulfill his "job" as a spiritual pilgrim to reach God? Does Jacob know he is a pilgrim? We think of Jesus telling Peter in the Garden of Gethsemane, "The spirit is willing, but the flesh is weak." We often let comfort or convenience stop us from experiencing the glorious adventure of a holy life.

Closing for Both Poems

Revisit the essential questions. You might use an app like Poll Everywhere to post anonymous student responses:

☐ How does "Finding a Box of Family Letters" connect us with the past? What wisdom does this poem share from the voices of the past?

☐ What does "The Burning Ladder" tell us about the benefits and costs of responding to God's invitation?

Writing Prompts for Both Poems

PHOTO INSPIRATION:

Pick an old photo. What do you imagine the people in it are saying and doing? Write a poem in which a present-day speaker reflects on the photo, imagining the voices of the past. In your poem, use alliteration, dialogue, and vivid sensory details that appeal to at least three different senses.

Teacher tip: Provide evocative historical photos. An online image search of "candid photos" with modifiers like "family," "meal," "baptism," and "jitterbug" can produce some useful options. You might also invite students to bring their own photos.

SCRIPTURE PASSAGE INSPIRATION:

Pick a scripture passage, such as the one in which the disciples fall asleep in the Garden of Gethsemane. Write a narrative poem inspired by the biblical text. What concrete details will build the story? What do you think the figures in this passage are thinking but not saying? Employ similes or other figurative devices for characterization. End the poem with a metaphorical line.

ESSAY OPTION:

Read "Ode to a Grecian Urn" by John Keats. In this poem, the speaker reflects on an object from the past. How do these two poems differ in tone? What wisdom does each speaker gain from contemplating objects in the physical world? Write a short essay comparing and contrasting how these two poems invite us to think about the passing of time.

Notes

1. Dana Gioia, "Poetry as Enchantment," *The Dark Horse*, 20th Anniversary Issue, Summer 2015, 8.

2. Gioia, "Poetry as Enchantment," 16.

3. Chi Luu, "How '*Carpe Diem*' Got Lost in Translation," *JSTOR Daily* (2019).

4. Hren, Joshua, "Climbing to God on "The Burning Ladder": Dana Gioia's *Via Negativa*," *Religion and the Arts* 23, no. 1/2 (2019): 124-141.

Lesson Two

WHAT LIES BEYOND THE SENSES

"The Road"

&

"The Lost Garden"

Objectives

1. Identify sonnet elements in a poem.

2. Interpret an extended metaphor.

3. Symbolically highlight a poem's meaning and poetic devices in a multimedia format.

4. Perform a poem with clear enunciation and effective inflection.

5. Discuss the explicit and implicit meanings of a poem.

Overview

Dana Gioia says:

> It is not enough to show the surface of the world
> or the exterior of existence. It is also necessary to
> reveal, or at least suggest, what lies beyond the
> physical senses. The relation between the visible
> and the invisible is an inevitable theme for the
> poet.[1]

In this lesson, we invite students to consider the relationship between the abstract and the concrete, as well as the writer's mission to convey Truth.

Memorization and Recitation

In memorization groups, students practice reciting the first quarter of their selected poems to one another. Make sure the students who are listening have the texts of the poems in front of them so that they can provide fruitful feedback to the student practicing recitation. Have each group member provide courteous and supportive feedback on pacing, inflection, expression, and accuracy.

Essential Questions

"The Road"

☐ *How does the poem develop the extended metaphor in the poem's title?*

☐ *How does the presence of unnamed characters create a sense of futility?*

☐ *What brings people happiness that is temporary?*

☐ *What makes us happy permanently?*

"The Lost Garden"

☐ *Who is the speaker in this poem?*

☐ *Which concrete descriptions produce an idealized setting in this poem? Which statements tinge the setting with regret?*

☐ *What can our nostalgia tell us about God's kingdom?*

☐ *What moments in earthly life do you think are closest to the joy of heaven?*

Literary Devices Introduced in This Lesson

DRAMATIC SITUATION—the plot element that presents a conflict the character(s) must face

EXTENDED METAPHOR—a comparison that is developed over the course of several lines to assist a reader in understanding abstract truths in familiar, concrete terms

TENOR—the thing or idea being represented in a metaphor

THEME—a universal statement that expresses an insight about the human condition

VEHICLE—the physical object used to represent the tenor in a metaphor

"The Road"

Context Setting

St. Thomas Aquinas tells us that only an infinite good (God) can satisfy our desire for human happiness. Worldly goods can only bring us incomplete happiness. Part of our life's adventure is to learn what eternal good is and to move our lives toward it. St. Augustine of Hippo expresses this yearning when he tells God, ". . . our hearts are restless til they rest in Thee."[2] When do you feel most at peace? Where do you find God in your daily life?

Vocabulary

Bewildered—confused; puzzled

Sloped—slanted

Body of the Lesson

Read aloud or invite students to read aloud "The Road." Then, explore the poem's extended metaphor together.

What do we miss in life because we are "far too busy looking for it [life]"? We miss meaningful relationships, joyful memories, personal growth, accomplishment of goals, and appreciation for life's blessings.

What is the tenor and what is the vehicle in this poem's central metaphor? We might frame the tenor as the good life, or a life well-lived, or the way to happiness. The vehicle is a physical road.

Where is the road meant to lead? Why is it sloped downhill? Life is meant to lead to heaven—to joy with God. Being sloped downhill might represent the easier path. We associate the phrase "going downhill" with this detail, and we think of a life sinking into despair, ruin, or even hell.

Why are the speaker and companions "bewildered to be there"? Is it good, bad, or neutral that "no one chose the way" and that "the path grew easier with each passing day"? The speaker and companions seem to have been living passively, allowing life to take them wherever it led, without mindfully choosing the good or disciplining themselves to work for a higher purpose. Perhaps they have thoughtlessly allowed themselves to be driven by their emotions and whims, not prioritizing what is most important.

DICTION

Pick out examples of strong diction. What emotional or abstract associations can you make with the words you've selected? Words like *drift, hazy, unaware, bewildered, downhill,* and *gloom* seem to convey passivity, confusion, lack of intellect, fear, sinking, and unhappiness.

THEME

How can this poem help us direct our lives to the ultimate good, to eternal Truth? We are reminded to appreciate the gifts of the moment, to actively—not passively—seek the highest good. Note the line "All seemed to drift by some collective will." Consider how the word "will" works ironically here to suggest *not* using our freedom of will properly. The poem urges us to prioritize clarity, gratitude, and attention to the moment. It reminds us not to passively follow trends, not to take the easy route, and not to be lured by lower goods, but, instead, to keep aiming for ultimate joy with God.

"The Lost Garden"

In the *Summa Theologica*, St. Thomas Aquinas tells us about something we all seek: perfect happiness, also called beatitude. Aquinas says, "Rational creatures (men and angels) seek God as the object that will fulfill them, and make them perfectly happy: God is their objective happiness. . . . The infinite beatitude of God perfectly embraces all beatitudes."[3]

The next poem is a poem of lost love. We might also read it metaphorically as a yearning for the paradise of the Garden of Eden. Despite its yearning tone of loss, the poem ends with a subtle expression of hope.

Vocabulary

Acreage—an expansive property

Gracious—courteous and generous-hearted; in Christianity, full of Divine grace

Mulberry—a plant that produces berries and can symbolize a time of abundance and beauty

Body of the Lesson

Read aloud "The Lost Garden" or invite a student to read aloud. Ask students to compare this poem thematically to "The Road." Note that the two poems share a wistful, nostalgic tone and a yearning for the beatific vision.

DRAMATIC SITUATION

Describe the poem's dramatic situation. The speaker reminisces about a romantic summer spent in the gardens of an old estate with "so many trees to kiss or argue under," reflecting on human pain and loss.

TONE

What tonal shifts and changes occur as the poem unfolds? The speaker conveys a sense of melancholy and nostalgia, as well as temporal distance from past pain. The speaker reflects on the "what-ifs" of the relationship, asking "What if we had walked a different path one day . . . ?" There seems to be a tone of regret or wistfulness in this musing. In the final stanza, the speaker seems to make peace with the present, "wanting nothing more than what has been." The final line takes on a hopeful and accepting tone, acknowledging that "the past [is] forever lost, yet seeing / Behind the wall a garden still in blossom."

CONTRAST

How does Gioia make use of contrast in this poem? Note the contrasts between past and present, ephemeral and enduring, kissing and arguing, pleasure and sadness. These contrasts convey the human tendency toward conflict and sorrow despite being endowed with abundant gifts. The contrasts also work to underscore the growth in suffering, the impossibility of "having it all," as the saying goes, and the endurance of lost love or past joy in the memory.

Where does the poem emphasize the "exterior" world, and where does it emphasize the "interior" world, as Dana Gioia suggested in the opening quotation? The garden's greenery on the old estate with its "gracious acreage of a grander age" serves as both exterior setting and symbols of an inner state. On a spiritual level, we might associate the motif of a lost garden with the Garden of Eden, of paradise lost by humankind as a result of the Fall. The hope at the end of the poem then might refer to the speaker's acceptance of lost love or, on a metaphysical level, the acceptance of human failings and a hope for future redemption and beatific joy, "seeing / Behind the wall a garden still in blossom."

FORM

Poets use **form** to give structure to their poems. You might think of form as the bones of a poem. Poet James Matthew Wilson explains how poetic form helps us "see" and communicate the highest good:

> Since antiquity, poetry has been understood above all . . . as a kind of *making* where talent and inspiration converge such that the divine and eternal finds expression through human ingenuity. The

central marker of this distinguished kind of making has always been *meter*, that practice of human speech where language is measured, brought to order, by a pattern that at once refines and deepens it, sets it apart from the everyday while also suggesting a connection with the order of reality as a whole.[4]

Let's see what kinds of measurements and moves poets make when they write a sonnet, the centuries-old, fourteen-line poem whose name means "little song" in Italian.

Students may benefit from reviewing this list of sonnet terms and characteristics:

COUPLET—two rhymed lines, one directly following the other

ENGLISH SONNET—three quatrains plus a couplet, with the rhyme scheme ABAB CDCD EFEF GG

FOOT—a unit of measurement in poetry

IAMB—a poetic foot with a weak-strong accent pattern

IAMBIC PENTAMETER—a line made up of five iambs

METER—the measured pattern of rhythmic accents in a line of verse

QUATRAIN—a four-line stanza

VOLTA—a turn in the poem's argument or tone

Have students work in small groups to identify sonnet characteristics in "The Road," such as the iambic pentameter, fourteen-line length, ABAB scheme of the third quatrain, and final couplet. Also have students point out characteristics of the poem that deviate from traditional sonnet form, such as the atypical rhyme scheme and the subtlety of the volta.

> *Active Learning Tip:* Help students feel the rhythm of iambic meter by dividing them into two groups and slowly reciting a few lines of the poem to them. One group can pound their desks as you recite each weak syllable. The other group can stomp the floor whenever you recite an accented syllable. The result should be a heartbeat rhythm: pound STOMP, pound STOMP, and so forth.

Closing for Both Poems

Revisit the Essential Questions for this lesson. You may wish to use the following questions in an Exit Ticket.

☐ *How can these poems help us aim for the highest good, not for lower goods that will ultimately leave us unsatisfied?*

☐ *If you composed a poem sharing what you've already observed about eternal Truth, what tone would you use? Would the poem's tone be upbeat, gentle, urgent, humorous, serious, or another choice? Why would you pick this particular tone?*

Writing Prompt and Projects

CREATIVE WRITING OPTION:

Write a poem titled "My Road" or "The Found Garden." In the poem, develop an extended metaphor to reflect on a life directed toward lasting joy.

POSTER PROJECT OPTION:

Have students create a poster visually representing the extended metaphor of "The Road" or "The Lost Garden." Ask them to highlight their favorite phrases or lines using images and quotes from the poem. Invite students to present their posters, explaining how they feel these images and lines create meaning in the poem.

INTERPRETIVE VIDEO OPTION:

Make a video interpretation of "The Road" or "The Lost Garden." The video should be at least 90 seconds long. In it, combine the spoken words of the poem with music and visual elements to convey the message of each stanza and to highlight the poem's dramatic force. Read the poem in the video with your own voice. Use music, lighting, colors, and images to creatively highlight shifts in meaning and tone.

Video Project Rubric Components

25%   Reads aloud the poem in a video at least 90 seconds long.

25%   Shows attention to detail in the video editing (sound, visual elements, and content).

25%   Selects music and visual images that reflect the meaning of each stanza.

25%   Creatively highlights shifts in tone and meaning.

Notes

1. Dana Gioia, *The Catholic Writer Today and Other Essays* (Belmont, North Carolina: Wiseblood Books, 2019), 127.

2. Augustine, *Confessions,* trans. F. J. Sheed, ed. Michael P. Foley (Indianapolis: Hackett Publishing Company, 2006), 3.

3. St. Thomas Aquinas, *Summa Theologica,* 1.26.1-4.

4. James Matthew Wilson, "Poetry in the Modern Age: An Editorial Statement," *Modern Age,* (Spring 2017): 8-9.

LESSON THREE

THE POWER OF BEAUTY

"God Only Knows"
&
"The Angel with the Broken Wing"

Objectives

1. Interpret the effects of rhythm, rhyme, allusion, fresh diction, narrative elements, and imagery in a poem.

2. Develop a distinct tone in a poem.

3. Infer theme and analyze characterization in a narrative.

4. Analyze the style a writer uses to create meaning in a poem.

5. Explain how details, diction, and imagery articulate the mood created in a poem.

Overview

Dana Gioia says:

> All art is incarnational. Art doesn't consist of abstractions. It is embodied truth created for creatures with bodies. A poem doesn't communicate primarily through ideas. It expresses itself in sound, images, rhythms, and emotions. We experience poems holistically. They speak to us simultaneously through our minds, our hearts, our imaginations, and our physical bodies. They speak to us, in other words, as incarnated beings.[1]

In this lesson we will consider the embodied truths contained in a carved piece of sculpture and in a music composition. The history of each work of art contributes to the truth it conveys.

Memorization and Recitation

In small groups, students practice reciting half of their selected poems to one another. Make sure students have the text of the poems in front of them when their peers recite so that they can provide fruitful feedback to one another. Each group member provides courteous and supportive feedback on pacing, inflection, expression, and accuracy.

Essential Questions

"God Only Knows"

☐ Which concrete details from the poet's imagination create a scene that feels "real" in this poem?

☐ How can the line length contribute to how fast or slow that readers experience a poem?

☐ When has music or a work of art brought you hope or healing? Have you ever seen a work of art that made you feel closer to God? Which one, and what about that artwork resonated with you?

☐ How can music and art connect us with God as Truth, Goodness, and Beauty Incarnate?

"The Angel with the Broken Wing"

☐ What details does the angel tell us about himself? Why are these details important for him to share with us?

☐ How does the angel convey his past, present, and future? What is his tone about each of these time periods?

☐ Imagine all that a historic cathedral or statue has seen. If these objects could talk, what wisdom would they impart?

☐ What incarnational characteristics are unique to religious objects? How would you describe the effects they cause within people?

Literary Devices Introduced in this Lesson

CONTRAST—dissimilarities that poets highlight to reveal a deeper truth

IRONY—a literary device in which the opposite of what is expected happens

STYLE—the way an author writes, including language, diction, syntax, and other elements that comprise what we often call a writer's voice

POINT OF VIEW—the perspective from which a story is told

SPEAKER—the imaginary voice speaking the words of a poem

"God Only Knows"

Context Setting

Mankind primarily experiences God through the three Transcendentals: Truth, Beauty, and Goodness, of which God is the ultimate expression. At its highest use, art reminds us of these characteristics and, thus, of God.

Incarnation is the mystery through which Divinity entered the human world as The-Word-become-flesh. The divine mystery continues to lovingly sustain the world in ways that the human person can perceive through the God-given gifts of intellect, reason, and perception.

According to the *Catechism of the Catholic Church* (paragraphs 457-459), The Word became flesh for us:

o   In order to save us by reconciling us with God

o   So that thus we might know God's love

o   To be our model of holiness

o   To make us "partakers of the divine nature."[2]

Vocabulary

Burghers—an archaic word referring to wealthy townspeople

Congregation—a group of people gathered to worship together

Improvised—made up on the spot

Ledger—a record of business transactions

Body of the Lesson

Invite one or more students to read aloud "God Only Knows." Ask students to share what they find unexpected in this poem.

IRONY

How does Gioia employ the unexpected to create meaning in this poem? The poem begins with a childlike tone, but in line six the poem takes a radical leap into imaginative space, perhaps highlighting our complacency and our tendency to misconstrue religion as trite. We often forget the glorious grandeur of God and the mortal battle being waged for our souls.

Poets use the unexpected to help us see truths that we often overlook. How does this poem help us see worship in a new light? In particular, how does this poem invite us to reflect on humility in worship? The final line reminds us of our fallen nature and that at church we are not singing insignificant nursery rhymes but are sending prayers to God "to save our souls." Eternity hangs in the balance; beautiful music, art, and architecture can help us experience the grandeur of God.

STYLE

What contrasting styles can you identify in this poem? The first stanza is a nursery rhyme. The poem uses short lines, conversational language, and a light, witty tone that leaves us surprised when the poem takes an apocalyptic turn.

How does Gioia use multiple styles to shift the tone and create a narrative arc? Summarize the narrative. What's happening in this poem? The poem progresses from childishness in the nursery rhyme, to dawning awareness when Bach's improvisation causes the burghers to sit up in their seats, to full awareness of the spiritual drama unfolding in and around them when they sing to save their souls.

THEME

What does this poem tell us about the salvific power of sacred music? How does this poem help us see the divine in the mundane? Music—its order, harmony, dynamics, etc.—can communicate God's beauty and mystery to us in ways we can't fully understand. We can come to know God better when sacred music lifts us out of the everyday and gives us a sense of the eternal.

"The Angel with the Broken Wing"

Context Setting

Dana Gioia says:

> We see the shape and feel the texture of
> things. We instinctively know that the form
> of a thing is part of its meaning. We are
> drawn to beauty, not logic. Our experience
> of the divine is not primarily intellectual. We
> feel it with our bodies. We picture it in our
> imaginations. We hear it as a voice inside
> us. We are grateful for an explanation, but
> we crave inspiration, communion, rapture,
> epiphany.[3]

Can you think of a moment when you had an experience of awe and wonder when listening to music or looking at a work of art?

Vocabulary

Ardor—passion

Docent—museum guide

Emblem—symbol of an abstract quality

Futility—having achieved nothing; pointlessness

Body of the Lesson

Read aloud "The Angel with the Broken Wing." If time permits, ask more than one student to read aloud.

Have students work in groups to find out what the poem conveys about the following thematic ideas: religious conflict, fear and hope of God, human denial of the divine, and the power of art. Each group should examine one thematic idea. Have the groups share their findings and discuss the connections among the ideas.

Students can work in small groups to identify literary devices that affect tone and mood in this poem, sharing their responses to the following questions:

DETAILS

Why does the angel describe himself first through what he is missing? What new significance does his missing wing take on at the end of the poem? The angel no longer serves in a church, where the faithful come to pray. He seems worn down and lonely for God. By the end, we find that he feels "nailed to a perch" and that he yearns to fly, to serve his sacred purpose and ascend beyond the flat secular world.

Talk about the line "I became the hunger that they fed." What hunger? Why did they feed it? What does the statue mean by saying it became that hunger? Perhaps the statue refers here to a hunger for God that the faithful fed through prayer because they yearned for God's healing and grace. The statue may embody our hunger for God, symbolizing humankind's desire for the Divine.

Why do you think the troops hit the statue "almost apologetically"? Perhaps they feel the deep transgression of desecrating sacred art because it conveys divine glory through beauty. Perhaps they discern a glimmer of the Divine in the statue and feel the burden of sin.

TONE

Discuss the use of contrasting qualities in diction such as "faith's ardor"/ "air-conditioned tomb" and "elegant" / "futility." We sense how out of place the angel is, severed from his sacred role. Instead of the role he is meant to serve, a glorious, divine service, he is now relegated to the basement as a stop on a museum tour.

What is the tone at the end of the first stanza and at the end of the second stanza? Which words convey a distinctive break between the tone of stanza one and two? How does the evolving tone used by the Angel affect the reader's mood as the poem progresses? At the end of stanza one, the angel sounds frustrated and constricted. At the end of stanza 2, the words "emblem of futility" convey a dejected irony. The following stanzas build in emotion as the angel remembers his past. Toward the end, he conveys an excited yearning, but the final line deflates this energy, and we feel the heartbreak of "faith's ardor" stifled.

Why did the poet choose the history of this character, the Angel, for this poem? The angel's history shows glimpses of humans in conflict, sorrow, and his present conveys a sort of secular lifelessness, as he stands in "an air-conditioned tomb."

What do you think are some of the things the angel wants to tell God? Perhaps the angel wants to tell God about the downtrodden and the suffering, "The hopeless [who] offered God their misery." Or, perhaps, the angel wants to communicate the pain of the souls who came through the church over the centuries: the lost and seeking, the cruel and broken, the saintly and hopeful.

Closing for Both Poems

Hold a brief wrap-up discussion:

☐ *How does music help you discern the eternal in the mundane?*

☐ *How can religious art transport us into dialogue with God?*

NURSERY-RHYME-TO-EPIC OPTION:

Take a nursery rhyme and expand it into an epic and unexpected narrative. In your poem, use humorous details to write about a meaningful topic. In the beginning, use diction and details to create a lighthearted or flippant tone. In the last stanza, use diction and details to create a tone of wonder and awe.

> *Advanced Challenge*: In your poem, use details to show–not tell, two contrasting tones. For example, Gioia references the "burghers / squirming in their pews" to convey their boredom and detachment, then later shows us "the roof / unbend itself" to illustrate the might, power, and wonder in Bach's musical "improvised / accompaniment / between two hymns."

STATUE MONOLOGUE OPTION:

Build a bank of individual words and/or phrases that might be used by a sacred statue to describe its history. Feel free to imagine the statue's "life" and what it has seen and heard. Make notes on how the statue felt when it was "young" and how it feels now. If you wish, incorporate other literary techniques you've seen in this unit, such as dialogue, a sonnet structure (partial or full), or an extended metaphor. Create a poem in which the speaker is a statue or building reflecting on all it has seen.

Kinesthetic Learner Challenge: Perform the poem to a series of live tableaux to interpret each stanza. If working individually, use digital or drawn images to create your tableaux. You may also create a graphic novel page to visually represent your poem.

POSTER PROJECT OPTION:

Either draw or select images on a digital or print poster to convey the details of "God Only Knows": the burghers in the pews, Bach at an organ, the roof unbending, the angels holding ledgers, the terrifying sky, and the congregation singing their hearts out. Add phrases from the poem to their posters and discuss their artistic choices.

ESSAY OPTION:

Write a persuasive essay using Dana Gioia's quotation "We are drawn to beauty, not logic." (See the full quote in the "Context Setting" section above.) Apply the quote to one of the two poems, or both, in this lesson to explore Gioia's insight about beauty and form.

Notes

1. Dana Gioia, *The Catholic Writer Today and Other Essays* (Belmont, North Carolina: Wiseblood Books, 2019), 164.

2. *Catechism of the Catholic Church,* second ed., Libreria Editrice Vaticana, 1994, 115-116.

3. Dana Gioia, "Christianity and Poetry," *First Things*, August/September 2022, 29.

LESSON FOUR

HOW SOUND INCARNATES MEANING

"Money"

&

"Pity the Beautiful"

Objectives

1. Compose poetry using genre characteristics and craft techniques.

2. Use literary devices such as anaphora, parallel structure, synonyms, colloquial language, direct address in a poem.

3. Analyze and use slang and irony in a lyric poem.

4. Analyze the impact of sonic devices in a poem.

5. Interpret the effects of irony, symbolism, rhyme, repetition, and accentual verse in a poem.

Overview

This lesson fosters engagement with sonic elements the poet uses to accentuate the poem's insights, and facilitates the rewarding experience of oral recitation.

Memorization & Recitation

In memorization groups, students practice reciting three quarters of each student's selected poem to one another. Make sure the students who are listening have the text of the poem in front of them so that they can provide fruitful feedback to the student practicing recitation. Have each group member provide feedback on pacing, inflection, expression, and accuracy.

Essential Questions

"Money"

☐ *How does the staccato force of one-syllable words affect the reader's experience of the poem?*

☐ *What should we value in life?*

☐ *What are the consequences of valuing the wrong things?*

☐ *How do enjambed lines control the poem's energy and movement in the first two stanzas?*

"Pity the Beautiful"

☐ *What fades in life, and what lasts?*

☐ *How can we anchor our lives to lasting things?*

☐ *How do the colloquial expressions influence the mood of the poem?*

Literary Devices Introduced in This Lesson

ANAPHORA—the repetition of a word or phrase at the beginning of successive clauses

COLLOQUIAL LANGUAGE—casual and conversational language

DIRECT ADDRESS—a technique in which the speaker of a poem talks to the reader

PARALLEL STRUCTURE—repeated sentence components

SLANG—unconventional, informal sayings that are often witty and clever

SYNONYM—a word that means the same as another word

"Money"

Context Setting

Try to recall a poem from your childhood that brought you great joy. You might remember reveling in poetry's sounds and images as a child. As we grow into adulthood, we can continue to love poetry with that same childlike glee. And loving poetry with joyful abandon, in turn, instills in us a love for the world around us because thinking like a poet helps us to see the world with fresh, appreciative eyes. Dana Gioia says:

> The central purpose of poetry is to praise existence—without, of course, denying the harsher realities . . . Wisdom comes from seeing and accepting reality—from understanding the vast beauty of creation and our own humble place in it. If poetry is to be a vehicle of truth and discovery, and not merely a pleasing fiction, then it must see, love, and praise the world, not as we imagine it but as it truly is.[1]

This poem gives us a chance to appreciate language's playful capacities and to discover the range of possibilities in poetic performance. Gioia reminds us that "poetry is a distinct category of language—a special way of speaking that invites and rewards a special way of listening."[2]

Vocabulary

Compound—a potentially lucrative investing practice

Body of the Lesson

Invite a student to read aloud "Money" or have them take turns reciting it to one another in pairs.

SONIC DEVICES

Can you recall a poem from your childhood that you enjoyed for its sounds as much as its meaning? After students recall poems from their childhood, invite them to savor the sounds of the clever poem "Money." Have students say some of the phrases to a partner, aiming to achieve the most appealing sounds. A few students might enjoy demonstrating for the class their best renditions of "the long green," "Greenbacks, double eagles, / megabucks and Ginnie Maes," or "greases the palm, feathers a nest."

What sonic devices does the poet use? Anaphora occurs in the lines "To be made of it!" and "To have it." Parallel structure connects the lines "Chock it up, fork it over, / shell it out. Watch it." Internal rhyme occurs with the words "cash" and "stash." One-syllable words almost exclusively comprise the diction of stanzas one and two, creating a rhythm that conveys the rhythm of dollar bills being counted.

SLANG

What are some of your favorite slang phrases in this poem? What do you find clever about them? Student answers will vary.

METAPHOR

What does it mean to "grease a palm"? This slang refers to bribery. Grease allows gears to turn smoothly and doors to open without squeaking. *How does money breed money?* Money invested results in interest earned.

DIRECT ADDRESS

Who is being addressed? The speaker addresses the reader directly.

What are the larger social issues that the poem calls into question? The poem draws our attention to the problems of greed, corruption, reckless spending, and failure to help those in need.

How does the pacing of the poem vary from stanza to stanza? Though the lines are shorter in the first few stanzas, the poem's pacing is slower in these lines. As the lines get longer, and the sense of money's circulation grows stronger, the pacing gains momentum, until the end, with a pause before the final resonant line.

What kind of "talking" does money do in the final stanza? How does the poet intend that a reader answer this question? The way we spend our money communicates what we value. It "talks" to the world about who we are. We are left with the sense that perhaps we should think about where we invest our money—as well as our energy, talents, and resources.

"Pity the Beautiful"

Poems are not a form of rational argument intended to convince a reader. Gioia says, "Poems are not so much about giving answers as about unfolding questions. . . . As a poet, I believe that what one leaves unsaid is often as powerful as what one says."³ The next poem, "Pity the Beautiful," implicitly poses questions for the reader. We'll infer those questions together and try to notice both what the speaker says and leaves unsaid.

Vocabulary

Adonis—in ancient Greek mythology, a strikingly handsome young man, favorite of the goddess Aphrodite

Apollo—the ancient Greek god of the Sun and archery; slang for a handsome young man

Blowsy—course and unkempt

Lousy—bad; disgusting; infested with lice

Body of the Lesson

Invite a student to read aloud "Pity the Beautiful." This poem also makes playful use of synonyms. Invite students to share their reactions to the variety of words used to describe "the Beautiful" and "the pretty boys."

SONIC DEVICES

Which sonic devices do you find most effective?
Student answers may include alliteration, assonance, meter, or rhyme.

Do you notice any sonic devices in this poem that were not used often in "Money"? This poem uses alliteration. There are also end-rhymes in lines two and four of each stanza.

DIRECT ADDRESS

What is the effect of direct address in this poem? How does the repetition impact the reader's engagement with the poem's ideas? These two devices add imperative force to the poem.

ANAPHORA

What is the effect of anaphora in this poem? It builds momentum. Note how the tone shifts slightly with each repetition.

How does Gioia make the repetition varied and dynamic, rather than dull and static? The third stanza breaks from the pattern. In the penultimate stanza, the imagery shifts to show faded beauty. The final stanza slows in pacing, the language becoming metaphysical.

Describe how each stanza feels a bit different and analyze how the poet builds significance as the poem progresses. The poem begins with playful language and a lighthearted tone, and ends with ethereal language and a metaphysical insight.

What is the impact of this shift? The shift in tone helps us reflect on the massive, typically unnoticed consequences of our choices, which are often shallow and thoughtless.

Closing for Both Poems

Have students fill out an Exit Ticket answering the following questions:

☐ *What is your favorite slang expression from today's lesson?*

☐ *What connection did you discover between slang and the literary device of metaphor?*

Writing Prompts and Activities

SATIRIC POEM OPTION:

Write two to four stanzas of accentual verse with rhymes on the 2nd and 4th lines of each stanza. In your poem, use irony to satirize one of the following: social media, consumerism, failure to care for the elderly, or cutthroat business practices.

> *Advanced Challenge*: Repeat a refrain but change one word. Use the technique of direct address. Another option is to make the poem an earnest song of praise instead of satire. If you choose this option, begin each stanza with a verb and its object, such as "Praise the . . ." and "Hold the . . ."

SLANG POEM OPTION:

Make a poem using all slang to contemplate a commonplace part of human life. Unfold a big-picture question in your poem.

> *Advanced Challenge*: In your poem, shift from the mundane or everyday to the divine or eternal.

PERFORMANCE CONTEST OPTION:

Hold a poetry recitation contest. In small groups of about four students, recite your poems to one another. Each group votes on one student to advance to the final round.

Finalists recite their poems in front of the class, and the class votes on the winner and a runner-up (or 1st, 2nd, and 3rd place winners). Teachers can offer winners bonus points on an assignment, a small prize, or bragging rights.

NOTES

1. Dana Gioia, *The Catholic Writer Today and Other Essays* (Belmont, North Carolina: Wiseblood Books, 2019), 144.

2. Dana Gioia, "Poetry as Enchantment," *The Dark Horse*, 20th Anniversary Issue, Summer 2015, 8.

3. Gioia, *Catholic Writer Today*, 161.

Lesson Five

SONGS OF PRAISE

"The End of the World"
&
"Psalm to Our Lady Queen of the Angels"

Objectives

1. Make connections to personal experiences, ideas in other texts, and society.

2. Evaluate the author's diction and syntax.

3. Write a poem using formal constraints.

4. Use and analyze metaphor, parallel structure, effective pacing, lists, participial phrases, and appositives in a poem.

5. Compose poetry using genre characteristics and craft techniques.

Overview

Featuring two contrasting poems, this lesson fosters reflection on pilgrimage, ancestry, community, and divine presence in the mundane. Students will reflect on their learning and on their engagement with the poems in this unit.

Memorization and Recitation

Plan a class day or event at which each student performs the poem they memorized for this unit. Grade the performance on pacing, physical stance, accuracy, volume, enunciation, expression, and inflection. You may also wish to have the student write out the poem to make it easier to grade the accuracy component.

Consider inviting audience members from the school community. Perhaps offer extra credit in a way that is appropriate for your students and classroom community.

Essential Questions

"The End of the World"

☐ *Who is the speaker of the poem?*

☐ *Where does the journey begin and where does it end?*

☐ *How is your life a pilgrimage?*

☐ *How does your life follow the hero's journey cycle?*

"Psalm to Our Lady Queen of the Angels"

☐ *How do the rhyming couplets add to the poem's peaceful ending?*

☐ *How does the poet use water to reflect the speaker's inner life?*

☐ *What cultural strength, heritage, and wisdom have you inherited from your ancestors? How can we better value the gifts and wisdom of the vulnerable and outcast?*

☐ *How do we speak to the saints to intercede for us? What is your song of praise?*

Literary Devices Introduced in This Lesson

ANAPHORA—repeated sentence or line beginnings

APPOSITIVE PHRASE—a noun set beside another noun to describe it, for example: "Holy Mary, Mother of God, pray for us sinners."

CHARACTERIZATION—details the author uses to portray character

EXTENDED METAPHOR—a comparison that is developed over the course of several lines to assist a reader in understanding abstract truths in familiar, concrete terms

PARTICIPLE—a form of a verb used as an adjective (present participles end with "ing," as in "*shining* sun"; past participles typically end with "ed," as in "*heated* pool")

PSALM—a sacred song or hymn

"The End of the World"

Context Setting

In Matthew 28:16-20, the risen Christ commissions the apostles to go throughout the world to preach and baptize. Part of the promise that Jesus makes is to be with those who preach his word: "Know that I am with you always, until the end of the world." As believers in the Divine Kingship of Jesus Christ, we can face the future with trust in God's providence. This poem can provide an opportunity to reflect on the mission to which God calls us in our mortal lives and on our eternal home with God.

Vocabulary

Tramped—to walk heavily

Dog-hobble—an evergreen shrub in the blueberry family

Osprey—a type of hawk

Eddy—to move in a circle

Ascend—to climb or rise up

Body of the Lesson

Read aloud or invite a student to read aloud "The End of the World" and, if time permits, Matthew 28:1-20. The Scripture passage complements this poem of journeying forth by reminding us that God is with us through our journeys and trials, when mentors guide us, and when we must proceed alone, even to the end of the world.

DICTION

Give examples of concrete action verbs that paint a picture of the scenes. "Scrambled," "Tramped," "streaked," "goosetailed."

What is your reaction to the words "the end of the world"? Student answers will vary.

Comment on the use of "we" as the subject, then the shift to "I." The speaker's guides have drawn back; he or she must venture forth alone. Our mentors prepare us to respond to the adventure of our life's calling; eventually, we are ready to venture forth as heroes of our own stories.

FORM

What choices has the poet made about form? The stanzas are quatrains, and each set of two lines is a rhymed couplet.

CHARACTERIZATION

What is the feeling of the narrator at the end of the poem? Does it appear that the narrator is a person of faith? "My journey done" has echoes of the phrase "well done" or "Well done, good and faithful servant," from Jesus's parable in Matthew 25:23.

"Psalm to Our Lady Queen of the Angels"

Context Setting

In speaking about his heritage, Gioia says: "I was raised by Italian and Mexican Catholics and attended Catholic schools for twelve years. . . . Catholicism is in my DNA— my ethnicity and my upbringing. . . . My sympathies are with the poor and the faithful—the people who raised me."[1] In addition to honoring his ancestors, Gioia also values tradition, saying:

> Poetry achieves its particular resonance by playing off the reader's experience with tradition. By "tradition" I don't mean any monolithic literary canon but rather the reader's total previous engagement with all sorts of literary texts—from nursery rhymes and popular songs to classic poems and novels. Those works set up a network of expectations and associations that provide contrasts and comparisons.[2]

Consider reading aloud "The Litany of the Blessed Virgin Mary" to students as an example of a religious list poem.

Vocabulary

Desecrated—violated

Destitution—poverty

Dispossessed—deprived of property and possessions

Mestizo—Spanish for "mixed"; used throughout Latin America to refer to a person of mixed ancestry

Mezzogiorno—Italian for "noon"; often refers to Southern Italy because of the hot midday sun there

Misbegotten—badly conceived

Body of the Lesson

Read aloud or invite a few students to read aloud "Psalm to Our Lady Queen of the Angels."

DICTION

How does Gioia's use of multiple languages contribute to the meaning of this poem? The multilingual nature of this poem contributes to its celebration of ancestors from many cultures who first settled the land and, over time, founded the city.

SHIFTS

Where does the poem shift to praise of the Blessed Virgin Mary? In the sixth stanza, the poem celebrates her and shows the people's reverence for her, communicated by "murals and medals, statues, tattoos."

ANAPHORA

Discuss the anaphora and its intended effects of emphasis and musicality in recitation. The final two stanzas build in intensity with the repeated sentence beginning, "Pray for us," followed by signs of brokenness and suffering. The prayer implores the intercession of the Blessed Mother, the "mother of the mixed and misbegotten," trusting in her care for "our desecrated city."

Look at the ways the poem describes the city. How do these words and phrases build an impression of the city for the reader? "Divided pueblo" in stanza six and *"city that lost its name"* in stanza eight convey that the city is suffering from disunity and a lost sense of self.

Closing for Both Poems

Having come to the end of the unit, students will benefit from stopping to reflect on their experience and their learning. Invite them to journal or respond to a survey with the following questions:

☐ *How have the poems in this unit spoken to you personally? What are your favorite lines, images, or details in the poems you studied?*

□ *What have you learned about your own poetic voice? What do you find most enjoyable about writing and reading poetry? What do you find most challenging?*

□ *How do you view poetry differently after your experience with these poems?*

Writing Prompts

NATURE WALK OPTION:

Go outside and spend time noticing the details of nature. Make a list of details. Write a journey of discovery in which you describe a journey through the natural world to the end of the world.

Advanced Challenge: If you can, compose each stanza of two rhymed couplets.

PSALM OPTION:

Write a psalm of praise to a saint using appositive and participial phrases. Pick one or two phrases or words to use with anaphora.

Multilingual Enhancement: If you speak another language, interweave phrases of that language into your psalm.

Notes

1. Dana Gioia, *The Catholic Writer Today and Other Essays* (Belmont, North Carolina: Wiseblood Books, 2019), 153.

2. Gioia, *Catholic Writer Today*, 150.

Bibliography

Aquinas, St. Thomas. *Summa Theologica*, 1.26.1-4. Claremont: Coyote Canyon Press, 2018.

Augustine. *Confessions*. Translated by F. J. Sheed. Edited by Michael P. Foley. Indianapolis: Hackett Publishing Company, 2006.

Catechism of the Catholic Church, second ed., Libreria Editrice Vaticana/USCCB, 1994.

Gioia, Dana. "Christianity and Poetry," *First Things*, August/September 2022.

Gioia, Dana. *The Catholic Writer Today and Other Essays*, Belmont, North Carolina: Wiseblood Books, 2019.

Gioia, Dana. "Poetry as Enchantment." *The Dark Horse*, 20th Anniversary Issue, Summer 2015.

Hren, Joshua. "Climbing to God on "The Burning Ladder": Dana Gioia's *Via Negativa*." *Religion and the Arts* 23, no. 1/2 (2019): 124-141.

Luu, Chi. "How 'Carpe Diem' Got Lost in Translation," *JSTOR Daily,* August 17, 2019.

Wilson, James Matthew. "Poetry in the Modern Age: An Editorial Statement." *Modern Age*, (Spring 2017): 8-9.

EDUCATIONAL STANDARDS
NATIONAL COUNCIL OF TEACHERS OF ENGLISH

1. Students read a wide range of print and non-print texts to build an understanding of texts, of themselves, and of the cultures of the United States and the world; to acquire new information; to respond to the needs and demands of society and the workplace; and for personal fulfillment. Among these texts are fiction and nonfiction, classic and contemporary works.

2. Students read a wide range of literature from many periods in many genres to build an understanding of the many dimensions (e.g., philosophical, ethical, aesthetic) of human experience.

3. Students apply a wide range of strategies to comprehend, interpret, evaluate, and appreciate texts. They draw on their prior experience, their interactions with other readers and writers, their knowledge of word meaning and of other texts, their word identification strategies, and their understanding of textual features (e.g., sound-letter correspondence, sentence structure, context, graphics).

4. Students adjust their use of spoken, written, and visual language (e.g., conventions, style, vocabulary) to communicate effectively with a variety of audiences and for different purposes.

5. Students employ a wide range of strategies as they write and use different writing process elements appropriately to communicate with different audiences for a variety of purposes.

6. Students apply knowledge of language structure, language conventions (e.g., spelling and punctuation), media techniques, figurative language, and genre to create, critique, and discuss print and non-print texts.

7. Students conduct research on issues and interests by generating ideas and questions, and by posing problems. They gather, evaluate, and synthesize data from a variety of sources (e.g., print and non-print texts, artifacts, people) to communicate their discoveries in ways that suit their purpose and audience.

8. Students use a variety of technological and information resources (e.g., libraries, databases, computer networks, video) to gather and synthesize information and to create and communicate knowledge.

9. Students develop an understanding of and respect for diversity in language use, patterns, and dialects across cultures, ethnic groups, geographic regions, and social roles.

10. Students whose first language is not English make use of their first language to develop competency in the English language arts and to develop understanding of content across the curriculum.

11. Students participate as knowledgeable, reflective, creative, and critical members of a variety of literacy communities.

12. Students use spoken, written, and visual language to accomplish their own purposes (e.g., for learning, enjoyment, persuasion, and the exchange of information).

NOTES

1. National Council of Teacher of English. *NCTE/IRA Standards for the English Language Arts.*